Cougar Club

The Initiation

Dark Chocolate

www.ManswellPeterson.com

Cougar Club: The Initiation

Copyright © 2013 by Dark Chocolate/Manswell T Peterson

ISBN: 978-0-9884351-4-8

Cover art designed by Gregory Graphics

All rights reserved. No part of this book may be reproduced or transmitted in any form or by any means, electronic or mechanical, including photocopying, recording, or by any information storage and retrieval system, without permission in writing from the copyright owner.

This is a work of fiction. Names, characters, places and incidents either are the product of the author's imagination or are used fictitiously, and any resemblance to any actual persons, living or dead, events, or locales is entirely coincidental.

This book was printed in the United States of America.

To order additional copies of this book, contact:

www.Amazon.com

In Memory of Mom

Rest in Peace. Thank you for your words of wisdom. I still hear them today.

AKNOWLEDGEMENTS

I want to thank the following people for all their support and help.

Rani Jones—My editor, thanks so much for helping me with this project. Even though you were up and down, you fought through it all to make sure that this was done and done very well. I can't thank you enough.
Brandie Randolph—My Editor, thank you as well for making sure this project was the Best.

Greg—Best cover designer in the World. As always Great Job!!!

In gratitude and love to my silent seven who were there with me from the beginning. You all kept asking for the return, and now I can say it is here…I hope I make you all Proud!!!

To all my fans from MySpace to Facebook, thank you for your emails, even the crazy ones. LOL.

To anyone I might have forgotten, I thank you also. Let's shock the world.

I love you all. Drop me a line some time.

Dark Chocolate

www.ManswellPeterson.com

Enter IF You Dare...

Dark Chocolate Man

CONTENTS

The Beginning

Shirley

Annette

Mary

Laverne

Sheila

Janice

Andrea

Bernice

Stephanie

The Cougar Club

****

Special Treat

The Beginning

As Shirley laid there feeling refreshed from the mind blowing orgasm she gave herself the night, she shook her head thinking about her encounter with Robert last night. She couldn't believe after telling this man over and over again how she needed to feel more sexual desire, he still was not able to satisfy her. Really, she thought crossing her arms and thinking about the debauchery.

She remembered when she first met him and the fire he put out in her. She had to be about 19yrs old. She didn't even know her body could explode like that. He taught her things that carried her throughout her adult years. He even showed her ex-husband a few things or two that he had taught her when she was younger… Remembering her sexual relations with her ex-husband gave her a tingle in between her thighs that she just hasn't gotten from Robert. She found herself smiling a bit until she thought of last night with Robert again.

Now he wasn't her man. She had a fling with him early in life. Recently, she ran into him at a gala and since both were single and available one thing lead to another. She was once again with the man who first brought her fire almost twenty years later and he can't do a damn thing to make her have an orgasm. What happened to the old Robert? He aged well. He now had that grown man look. A Billy Dee or Denzel type look. He owned three dealerships in the Atlanta area. He was divorced, 50yrs old, and a he was a real catch for someone, well for someone who didn't care about sex.

She spoke to him about his stamina last week when he disappointed her. He tried over and over again to make her cum but he just couldn't stay alert. His eating

skills were poor. She gave him a straight up "F".

He seemed to really want to make their sexual relationship work. He paid close attention to her instructions she gave. He tried practicing on a peach eating pussy all week. He even got a prescription for the little blue pill.

She was so excited to get his call because she really enjoyed his company and was curious to see what he had learned. He said he was ready and she should get prepared. He told her Viagra was supposed to take their sexual relationships to a whole new level, but look at this mess.

He literally pumped her six times and half ate at her pussy. He was so excited she thought it was his anxiety. She did everything to get him back up but now she is just pissed. Who falls asleep while someone is sucking your dick? This shit was just too unbelievable to her.

Yeah he beat the pussy up shaking her head she

thought to herself. He put that shit to sleep, in a coma.

. He took the lead as soon as she opened the front door. Her pussy instantly started jumping when he grabbed her by the waist and gave her a long deep kiss. This was going to be a night to remember. It was like something out of a movie, clothes flying off and almost tripping over each other trying to get to the bedroom.

He pushed her on the bed, Shirley loved it. It was wild. Her juices were flowing. She grabbed at him attempting to pull him on the bed with her so she could suck him off just a little. "No, this is all about you baby!" Robert said. Shirley smiled as he gently laid himself on top of her.

He planted kissing from her collarbone down to her feet. He sucked each toe. This foreplay was more than she was expecting. She didn't complain she just enjoyed this pleasure. He slowly kissed back up playing close attention to the area behind her knees. Oh yes, she said to herself, most men miss this spot. "Do it, daddy." Shirley said moaning lightly. This was everything she desperately needed and wanted. Then he slowly rose to her pussy.

A few sloppy wet kisses on her pussy mound, six pumps, a rollover, and just like that it was over. What just happened?

"Damn baby wasn't that good? Robert said as he sank into a pillow getting comfortable. "Umm, Hell no! What was that? Are we done?" Shirley said looking at him like he was crazy.

"Baby I tried my best, I mean I came and it's going to be a minute before I can go again."

"Like hell you did. You supposed to be able to go for hours on that pill. Here let me suck your dick some and then we can start over."

"Ok!"

Shirley went to work on that dick licking and slurping like this was her last meal. Her hormones were on fire. She was hoping to start the night over. Maybe a little slower would help. Then she heard snoring. Robert was snoring like a baby who just got full of his momma milk and had a fresh diaper change.

She had had enough. Finally shaking her head, she screamed "That's it! I have had enough. I am sick and tired of not getting satisfied. Get up, get out of my bed. I can do better with my toys. My finger last longer. My toys have a better lifespan than you do!"

"What do you mean? Babe, come on now, we at that age where stuff don't always function right. I mean I got
the Viagra for you. I just forgot to take it. Get me some water; I will be up in no time."

"Are you serious? You forgot to take it? You forgot that I was in this bed with you, and you forgot that I NEED SATISFACTION TOO, you are an old fart. You started off like you were going to do something, then nothing! Go, get your mess and leave, get out my house!"

As Robert gathered his clothes, he stopped trying to explain anything to Shirley. She was right, he had it coming. This wasn't the first time. He didn't know whether to be embarrassed or ashamed. As he walked toward the door, he turned and said these words: "Maybe you should just get you one of those young bucks that got that stamina thang and can just go for hours and will do all those freaky thangs you like, Shirley, cause God knows I just can't do all that stuff, I am too old and ain't got time for that freaky stuff."

"Well maybe I will just do that!" With that, Shirley door closed.

Shirley was steaming partly because she was horny and the other part because Robert was right. They were at that age where sexual relationships were dead or slowly dying. Being near fifty was nothing like twenty-five. Yes, it was advantages such as financial stabilities but that didn't make up for those lonely unsatisfying nights. Men became more selfish as they got older and women basically just learned to cope with whatever they were given. If only I could get that sexual gratification I
had when I was young. I bet my friends are going through this same thing, she thought as she flipped on the TV.

As she sat there and watched Tom Cruise jump up and down like a damn fool on TV because he hooked up with that little young girl Katie, Shirley had an idea.

Robert had just said she needed a young

buck; Tom Cruise is acting a fool over his young pussy, what the hell she remembered Demi Moore got her a young one too. She wasn't trying to marry anyone; Shirley merrily wanted to be satisfied. She knew her friends had this same problem, why not form a club of older women being satisfied by young dick swinging horny young men. We could help each other out? She knew her friends were on the more conservative side. Very southern or proper and no one would just bite so she would have to test it out beforehand. If I set the pace, the freakiness will come out of those gals. Every woman deserves to be pleasured to her own terms of satisfaction.

Getting older was a part of life. Most people get better with time but this was ridiculous. She now knew she was never going to go through anything like this again. She knew what she needed to do.

What a wonderful idea she thought as she turned off the TV and pulled out her toy. She was so turned on by the thought of having her way with a young guy; she had her first orgasm in months. Cougar Club she said softly as she drifted off to sleep.

Shirley finally arose from the bed remembering the name Cougar Club. It had a nice ring to it. She was eager to get started. She thought about what she would need and who she would invite to be a member of it. She felt it necessary to compile a list but she had a flight to catch and she was late. Guess I have something to do on the plane she thought as she hurried to take a shower and get ready for her flight.

Shirley's Story

Shirley Henderson

Shirley is 47 years old. She is the owner of a staffing agency. Her back ground is business administration and she is a former colleague of Mary Johnson. Shirley has been divorced for seven years. She has a son who is 25 and a daughter who is 23.

Shirley Henderson

Everyone was yelling and screaming. Barack Obama had just been elected President of the United States of America. Shirley was happy and excited. She went to the bar to get another drink. Once there, she placed her order and asked a gentleman sitting there "Is this seat taken?"

The moment they made eye contact, Shirley knew this was the beginning of her Cougar Club and her world would never be the same. The gentleman extended his hand and said "Hi, my name is Tyrone...and you are...?" Shirley looked over and saw his deep dark eyes. "Shirley" she said.

The two of them shared a very intimate conversation about politics and how things had changed. Shirley knew this young man was at least 15 years younger but at this moment she didn't care. He was flirting with her and she was flirting back. Shirley looked at him and decided to take the conversation to a whole new level.

She asked the young man what would it take for her to have his company the entire night. Tyrone took a sip of his drink, put his glass down at the bar, he just knew Shirley was joking. He turned his head, looked at her and said "$400."

Shirley looked at him before uttering, "That's kinda cheap for a good-looking man like yourself." She could not believe she was offering money for sex and telling him to raise his price. What she did know what this was the type of guy her body was longing for. She knew this

was her perfect opportunity to start her club and this was the perfect test. Tyrone then stated "Okay, Big Baller, make it $500."

Shirley finished her wine and told him

"Wait, right here," then she smiled and winked at him, "I'll be right back."

Tyrone watched Shirley as she walked away and he had to admit to himself she was a gorgeous woman. She had a nice ass on her. His life had been turned upside down so why not have a little bit of great sex on election night. Then to top it off she wanted to pay him. Yeah, this was going to be a great night he thought.

Shirley returned about five minutes later and she handed Tyrone a key to the room they would be sharing that evening. She leaned over to his ear and whispered "There are several rules if you want to follow them and this will be a night you won't forget! Give me ten minutes and then come up to this room."

Tyrone sat at the bar contemplating whether to go up to the room or just go home. But he thought to himself, *'what's home? My wife and my kids are gone. Tomorrow, my job will be gone....what else do I have to lose?'* He finished his drink and went to the elevator. He stepped off on the 17th floor and opened the door. He had no idea what was in store for him.

Walking into the room, Tyrone heard very soft music playing in the background. All of the lights in the room were turned off. He could hear Shirley's voice coaxing him "Come over to the bed." Tyrone walked over to the bed as Shirley had commanded "take off your clothes but do it nice and slow." There was no doubt she was going to be in control tonight.

Tyrone slowly removed his clothes. Shirley became
hornier. She began to slowly rub herself and then she reached over, grabbed his penis with her left hand and said "Come to Momma." Her eyes fixated on

how large his penis was as she grabbed his balls with her right hand. She played with his balls with her right hand and then she told Tyrone to put one leg up on the bed.

Now she had full access to his balls and she continued to play with them with her right hand. As she played with his dick and his balls, Tyrone's eyes closed from the sheer pleasure of what she was doing. For years, he had to beg his ex-wife to do these things and a majority of the time, she refused.

Shirley leaned forward and she slowly played with Tyrone's dick, licking her tongue at the top of his penis and massaging the opening with the tip of her tongue. Tyrone was going crazy. Shirley was still massaging his balls with her right hand and now she had the head of
his penis in her mouth. She was sucking and slurping and getting excited because of the way his dick

was jumping. She then decided to nibble on his dick -- not too hard but not too soft. She could see Tyrone's legs were about to buckle from the pleasure she was giving him for she knew she had him at that moment.

She put the entire dick in her mouth. Tyrone begged her to let him make love to her. Shirley refused to stop. She kept going. She would pull his dick in and pull it out. Pull it in and pull it out. The pleasure Tyrone was feeling had him trying to move with Shirley but she wanted to be in control. She reached her left hand around and grabbed Tyrone's ass forcing him to stop bucking. She was rubbing his ass, sucking his dick, and playing with his balls. Just as Tyrone was about to have an orgasm Shirley stopped sucking him and climbed back further in the bed.

Tyrone began to make his way towards Shirley

but right before he could get completely on the bed, Shirley put her foot on his chest. She told Tyrone to remove the shoe from her foot. Tyrone grew more excited as he undid the strap to her shoe. Once Shirley's foot was completely out of her shoe, she told Tyrone to suck her toes. She did this with a devilish look on her face and Tyrone obliged her.

Tyrone put the big toe in his mouth at first, running his tongue from side to side. He was getting turned on by the mere smell of her body. He tried to put her whole foot in his mouth. He was sucking her big toe all the way to the pinkie toe...nibbling and sucking...nibbling and sucking.

Shirley was rubbing her pussy with her one hand and her titties with the other. Tyrone took off his boxer shorts and climbed into the bed with Shirley. He moved

up in bed closer to Shirley and just as he was

about to climb on top of her, she stopped him.

She told Tyrone he had to take his time, "Show a woman that you appreciate her, get her body all warmed up before you try to take it for a drive."

Tyrone was learning how to make love to a woman. Shirley moved Tyrone's head to her vagina and told him "I want you to eat me first and take your time."

Of course Tyrone was like any other guy,. He licked the pussy for about two minutes and then he tried to stick his penis into her vagina. Shirley once again had to slow him down. She told him to lick her pussy as if it were an ice cream cone. She told him to follow these instructions with any woman he made love to and she would beg him not to stop. Shirley opened up her legs wider. She pulled her pussy lips apart and showed Tyrone where her clit was. She instructed him to put his lips right there as if he were kissing a woman on the mouth. As Tyrone began to lick Shirley, the little pink head of her clit began to poke out. She told Tyrone, "This is what you want to do," as she pointed to her clit and made him observe the swollen little pink head that had poked out of her clit. Tyrone put his face back in the middle of her pussy and began licking her clit. Shirley had an orgasm. She grabbed the back of

Tyrone's head and squeezed it tighter to her pussy. She hadn't realized how horny she was getting teaching this younger man how to eat pussy.

Before she realized it, Shirley had another orgasm. She pulled Tyrone up and as he put his penis into her pussy, Shirley had another orgasm. Tyrone was clearly turned on by this time. He wanted to stroke her hard and fast. He was ready to have an orgasm himself but as he began to go faster and faster, Shirley stopped him again. She explained to him that once a woman has an orgasm she is still hot and ready to go, sometimes for hours, and if he took his time, he could be one of the best lovers she ever had. Tyrone then slowed down and began to make love to Shirley. As he did this he noticed how eager she was to allow him to go deeper into her pussy. Shirley lifted her legs higher and higher with each stroke of Tyrone's penis. She moaned out loud "Damn, I'm cumming again!"

This turned Tyrone on more and as Shirley lifted her legs up, he could feel the tension in her thighs. Her toes were pointed up directly at the ceiling. Tyrone couldn't hold it any more. He started shooting an orgasm deep into Shirley's pussy. Shirley could feel Tyrone's dick throbbing with every burst of juice he set inside her. Once Tyrone finished having his orgasm, he sat up and Shirley slowly turned onto her stomach. Shirley explained to

Tyrone that what she was about to teach him would turn any woman out completely and he would have a love slave for life.

Shirley got on her hands and knees and told Tyrone to eat her pussy from behind. Tyrone began licking her pussy lips as Shirley yelled out "Damn baby, eat that pussy.... eat that pussy! Oh shit, I'm cumming again," and with that, Shirley had another orgasm and she squirted juices all over Tyrone's face. Tyrone had never had a woman do that to him and he grew more excited.

Shirley opened her ass up and told Tyrone to run his tongue from the bottom of her pussy up to her ass. She told him to stick his tongue in her ass. Tyrone was so turned on that he almost had another orgasm. As he stuck his tongue into Shirley's ass, her juices started to drip all over the bed again. This drove Tyrone crazy.   She then said in a sweet voice, "Have you ever had anal sex with a woman?"

Tyrone said nervously, "I have always wanted to...but never did."

Shirley reached under the pillow and grabbed a small tube of lubricant. She told Tyrone where to put the lubricant and told him to rub some all over his dick. She told him to slowly work his dick into her ass. Tyrone began to see his dick disappear into Shirley's ass. He got so excited he had an orgasm. Shirley could feel his juices being shot up in her and she had an orgasm at the same time. They both collapsed on the bed and lay there and talked.

Tyrone and Shirley talked and got to know one another, Tyrone explained he had lost his job due to bad economic times. He continued talking explaining how his wife left him but he told her he wasn't looking for a pity party.

He asked her why she was single and Shirley

explained how she was tired of all the pill popping, Viagra-taking men who were trying to date her. She told Tyrone no longer would she date a man who would not eat pussy for more than ten minutes nor would she date a man that couldn't get his dick hard. Tyrone looked at her, scooted up closer to her and told her she deserved the best and with that, he put his arms around her and they both just listened to the music and drifted off to sleep.

The next morning Tyrone was awakened by the sounds of Shirley's keys as she was preparing to leave. He reached out to her and she grabbed his hand, he told her "You don't have to go yet."

Shirley smiled back and told him she had to go as she had a company to run and it wasn't going to run
itself. And with that, Shirley gave Tyrone a kiss on the forehead and walked out the door. Tyrone

jumped out of bed smiling about his previous night and laughing to himself about this older woman who had just ran game all over him. As he took his shower he couldn't help but think about the things Shirley made him do. He had never licked a woman's ass before. What was it about her that made him do it? Was it how beautiful she was? Was he just caught up in the moment?

The pussy was damn good. He just couldn't understand why he did those things. The more he thought about it, the harder his dick got and he began to fantasize about fucking Shirley in the ass. He slowly began to jack his dick and found himself stroking faster and harder with every thought about her. Before he knew it, he had shot his love juice all over the shower; the hot water was still running all over his body. For the first time, in his life, he had jacked off and his dick stayed rock hard.

After completing his shower, Tyrone got dressed and was about to leave the hotel room when he noticed an envelope with his name on it by the door. He opened up the envelope and inside were five $100 bills and a check for $1,000 along with a note that stated,

Hey love, had a wonderful time last night. Never sell your worth for less than what you are. Here's my card. Call me tomorrow after 5:00 pm.

Shirley

Tyrone had forgotten all about the arrangement for the money. He had such a good time he figured he should pay her.

But he also knew he needed the money because of his job situation. He stuck Shirley's card in his shirt pocket along with the money and check and walked out the door.

Later that day, Shirley's flight took her back to Atlanta. She'd had a wonderful time in Chicago but now it was back to work. Throughout her work day, she thought about how she had dominated Tyrone and how much it turned her on to do so. She knew he would call even though he would try to play it off and be Mr. Cool. She knew he would be perfect for her club. He was the definition of boy toy. He was handsome, smart, available, and very teachable. Best thing was, he was eager to learn.

Shirley decided she would go to her favorite after work drinking spot for happy hour and wait and see if Mr Tyrone would call. Later that evening, as Shirley was sipping an apple martini, her cell phone rang. It was Tyrone. Shirley's nipples became hard at just the sound of his voice. She even felt her pussy get wet thinking about that young face and how she pushed it deep into her pussy.

Tyrone and Shirley talked for about 45 minutes and during the conversation she asked him how the job search was going. He told her horrible as there were no jobs in Chicago at that time. He joked with her mentioning that if she had a boy toy position available he would take that. Bingo Shirley thought. Shirley told him that the position he asked about was available but he needed to come to Atlanta to acquire it. Tyrone told her he could be there in a week's time as he had to tie up some loose ends.

The phone conversation ended and Tyrone called a few of his Atlanta buddies and told them he needed a couch to crash on for a couple of weeks until he got himself situated. They all agreed after Tyrone told them when he would be driving to Atlanta. Some of his boys volunteered to help him find a job but he told them he had that all under control.

One week later, as Tyrone adjusted to his new home of Atlanta he decided to pop in and see Miss Shirley and check on the job offer she had made. Tyrone was a little lost trying to drive around downtown Atlanta and was very grateful for the new GPS his boys had purchased for him. He didn't know what excited him the most, moving to the new city or the thought of seeing Miss Shirley and wondering if they would have anymore encounters.

Annette's Story

Annette Wilson

Annette is 48 years old and she has been divorced for six years. She is a Federal Court judge, the youngest female to be appointed to the Federal bench ten years ago at the age of 38. Annette has one son, aged 24, who is in grad school.

Annette Wilson

"Okay Shirley, whatever you're doing and whatever has you glowing like that, I want some of it," Annette said when she came into Shirley's office for a quick visit. Shirley looked at her, with a devilish smile on her face, and stated "Girl, are you sure you can handle some of what I'm getting? Last time I checked you had put yourself on lock down because you're Miss Federal Judge" she laughed.

Annette looked at her and shook her head and said, "No, I got to get me some of that. I am tired of being horny. Are you willing to share what you got?" Annette said jokingly.

Shirley was twirling a pen in her hand thinking she could be my second member of the club and she looked back at Annette and asked "Are you serious?" Annette shook her head and said "HELL yes!"

Shirley asked about her schedule for the week. Annette grabbed her calendar and showed it to Shirley. Shirley marked off a two hour time block for the next day and as she handed the calendar back to Annette, she explained "There are some rules to this girl and you must abide by them. No ifs, ands, or buts."

Annette sat up in her chair eagerly listening and waiting for Shirley to begin giving her the rules.

Shirley looked at her and said "Remember YOU asked me for this, okay.

"One -- you do whatever is asked of you. Two -- you can't say no. Three -- enjoy yourself. I've marked your calendar just so you'll remember. I will send you an angel and I promise you he will take you to heaven."

While Shirley and Annette continued to talk Annette's phone rang. It was her clerk at the courthouse. Annette stood up, gave Shirley a hug and told her "Girl I got to go back to the office. I'll catch up with you later." Annette walked out and Shirley mumbled to herself *'you will catch up, that I promise.'*

Annette exited the elevator as Tyrone was entering the elevator. He got a good look at Annette and his mind began to race as he looked at her from head to toe. He vacated the elevator on Shirley's floor. The lingering smell of Annette's perfume drove him crazy. Tyrone told the receptionist he was there to see Miss Shirley. She told him to have a seat and Shirley would be right with him.

Tyrone looked around Shirley's company. He had no idea the company was so huge. While he was glancing at the artwork, Shirley came around the corner and invited him to her office. Shirley and Tyrone shared several minutes of small talk then he asked her about the job. She explained to him he would do odds and ends around the office but she was going to use his special talents in other locations. Shirley got up from her desk and walked around to where Tyrone was sitting. She leaned on her desk and asked him would he do her a huge favor.

Tyrone responded "Yes, anything for you."

Shirley explained to him about Annette and how she wanted him to go to her office and ravish her completely. She explained to Tyrone that she wanted

Annette to be on the verge of collapsing from great pleasure. Tyrone asked her "Are you sure you want me to go over there and have sex with your girlfriend?"

Shirley interrupted and told him "No, not go over there and have sex, I want you to go over there and make love to her as if your life depended on it."

Tyrone agreed and Shirley pulled out an

envelope from the top drawer of her desk and handed it to Tyrone. Tyrone opened the envelope and counted the money. He looked at Shirley and said "Fifteen hundred dollars?"

Shirley looked at him and said, "I can't have my boy toy struggling. Oh yes, $1,500 dollars for one afternoon of work."

Tyrone stood up, gave Shirley a hug, and just as he was about to kiss her, she stopped him, inches from her

lips, and handed him another envelope. She briefly explained the contents of the second envelope and told him another set of instructions were inside but he couldn't open the envelope until he got to his location. Tyrone agreed and Shirley kissed him and told him goodbye.

The next day Annette was at her office going through her normal routine but she found herself continually staring at the clock eagerly waiting to find out what Shirley had set up for her. She wondered aloud what it could be that she couldn't say no to but yet she had to fully participate. The time was 10:55 am and Shirley had

blocked off 11:00 am to 1:00 pm. Annette had given her staff a two hour lunch break so they would not interrupt what was about to happen. As Annette stared at the clock and daydreamed a sudden knock on her door brought her back to reality. She sung out "Come in. It's open." and in walked Tyrone locking the door behind him as he entered.

Annette jumped up from her chair and asked the stranger "May I help you?"

Tyrone looked at her with a smile on his face and said "Shirley sent me."

Annette swallowed and her nipples became hard. She remembered seeing this man yesterday as she was leaving Shirley's office. Even though she was turned on, she told the man "There must be some mistake."

Tyrone walked closer to Annette. He put a finger over both of his lips motioning her to be quiet. He then
moved Annette's chair and he stood directly behind her. He touched her shoulders and she immediately became wet. She could smell his cologne and it was sexually intoxicating. He leaned over and whispered in her ear, "There is no mistake here…only the pleasure I am about to give you."

Tyrone kissed her neck right below her right ear. Annette got goose bumps from the slow kiss. She felt her pussy start to throb. She was frozen in time as this younger man with soft delectable lips began kissing her all over her neck. He reached around with both hands and slowly began to massage her breasts. He could tell she was turned on by the way her nipples had responded.

He moved stuff around on her desk and gently bent her over asking her to spread her legs and Annette

obliged him. She was wondering what she was doing. Of all the places and of all the times -- why here and why now? Tyrone began to rub her butt with both hands. With every touch Annette was turned on more and more. Her pussy was throbbing even more. For the first time in her life she was not in control of the situation. She began to moan softly as Tyrone lifted up her skirt and continued to rub her butt, gently gliding his hands over her pantyhose. He leaned over and kissed both sides of her butt and began rubbing her thighs. Annette felt like she was going to explode.

He pulled down her pantyhose along with her panties and he asked her to step out of them. Once again, Annette obliged him. He slipped her shoes back on and got on his knees. Tyrone began to kiss her ass again -- one cheek and then the other cheek. He then rubbed her pussy and Annette moaned even louder. He gently opened her legs further and began licking her pussy lips.

The anticipation was too much for Annette and she had an orgasm as he rubbed his tongue over the outer part of her lips. Tyrone continued to lick her lips and slowly made his way to her clit. There he was clit to face, pushed between the ass cheeks of Annette, and he was enjoying every minute of it. Annette wanted to turn around to give him a better angle of her pussy but he told her to stay right there in that position.

After about twenty minutes of licking her from behind, he turned Annette around. As she leaned against the edge of her desk with Tyrone on his knees, he began to lick her pussy again. Annette's eyes rolled to the back of her head and as she reached around and grabbed his head with one hand, she was stunned and amazed she was having multiple orgasms. The more Tyrone licked her, the hotter each orgasm became. Annette was having

one continuously long orgasm. Her juices would not stop flowing. After a couple more orgasms she yelled out "Oh shit!"

Tyrone stood up and he pushed her body so she was laying flat on her desk. He dropped his pants and positioned his dick in the opening of Annette's pussy. As he pushed the head deep into her pussy,

Annette moaned louder. Tyrone was enjoying this tight pussy and almost had an orgasm himself. Finally, he eased all of himself in Annette's pussy. Reaching up with his left hand he grabbed her hair.

He reached up with his right hand and grabbed her shoulder. He began to long stroke Annette and she enjoyed every bit of it having orgasm after orgasm after orgasm after orgasm. But before Tyrone began having orgasms himself he pulled his penis out and began to lick Annette's pussy again. She had another orgasm.

He placed his hands across both of her butt cheeks and he spread her ass open. He then began to lick the crack of her ass and Annette moaned in pleasure all over again. No man had ever licked her like this before and it was driving her crazy. Tyrone pulled out a tube of lubricant and spread it all over his dick.

He then took some of the lubricant and put it right on the crack of Annette's ass. Annette did not know what to think at this moment. This younger man had made her so horny she couldn't say no to anything he wanted to do to her. As Tyrone placed his penis in position to enter Annette's anal cavity he could tell she was getting excited. She was squeezing her butt cheeks and the lubricant was going in and out with every squeeze, and then it happened, he slid the head of his dick into her ass and she moaned like she never moaned before.

Tyrone slowly worked his penis deep into Annette's ass and he kept reminding her to breathe and relax. The pleasure was too much for Annette. Her body was going limp and she enjoyed every bit of it. Tyrone could not hold back any further. He was about to have an orgasm deep in her ass and

Annette was moaning louder and louder with each stroke of his dick. With a couple more pumps of his dick in her ass, Tyrone began to grunt. Annette could feel his dick starting to throb and vibrate as Tyrone shot his load deep inside her.

He collapsed his body weight on top of her with his dick still deep in her ass. Annette tried to get up but Tyrone wouldn't let her. He held her hands and began to pump nice and slow. As he pulled his dick out of her ass Annette began to moan even louder. Tyrone walked to her private bathroom and cleaned himself up. Once he
was finished he walked back out to see Annette still positioned across her desk. He reached into his pocket and handed her an envelope. He told her to go clean up before she read the envelope. Annette stood up. Her legs were wobbly, her nipples were hard, and her pussy was throbbing. After a few

minutes in the bathroom, Annette walked back out.

She smiled at Tyrone and opened up her envelope. She pulled out the note and a business card fell on her desk. She picked the card up and noticed it had two C's on it. One was a sparkling silver C; the other was a sparkling gold C. She turned the card around and read the note on it. It stated:

Welcome to the Cougar Club. You passed your initiation.

Shirley

Tyrone winked at her before he left her office. The only thing Annette could do was to sit back in her chair and smile. Once Tyrone returned to his car, he sat down and he called Shirley to let her know how things had gone. She was pleased to hear the good news.

She asked him "How did she look when you left?" with a giggle in her voice. Tyrone answered "She will never be the same. I feel sorry for the next man who comes along in her life." Shirley told Tyrone to make sure he stopped by her office to pick up his paycheck. Tyrone was a bit confused and reminded her that she had already paid him but Shirley told him that was for the job he had just completed and the new check was for the running around he did for her company. Tyrone murmured to Shirley "I could get used to this" and he hung up the phone.

Shirley called Annette to check on her to see how she was doing. Annette finally answered the phone once she realized it was Shirley on the other line.

She answered laughing "Girl, where did you find him? He did things to me I only read about in those crazy books!"

Shirley told her he was a friend and an employee with those special talents that he had. Shirley then mentioned "You did say you wanted that glow that I have, right? Well, what you just got is the reason for my glow."

Annette asked Shirley what was the Cougar Club?

Shirley explained "the Cougar Club was a group she was

forming consisting of older women who were tired of the pill-popping, Viagra-men, and all those other men who have problems getting their dicks hard...so you see what we are doing is the same thing that older men do.

They date younger women 'cos it makes them feel

alive, young, and vibrant.

"We date younger men because we get to have great sex and to feel worshipped by them. That's what we do in the Cougar Club. Some of these men could be as young as 15 to 20 years younger than us. We just don't care anymore.

"I know me personally I refuse to have sex without enjoying it anymore! And from what you just got, do you think you can go back to the old ways of having sex?"

On the other end of the telephone Annette shook her head and said "Girl, hell to the naw. I have never been licked and fucked so much in my life. I will definitely have to find me some more young meat to keep me satisfied.

"So who else is in the Cougar Club besides us, now that I am a card-carrying member?" laughed Annette.

Shirley told her "It's two of us now with two more initiations taking place this weekend. One lady will get a big surprise at her conference Saturday morning. They both said the same thing you mentioned about my glow and that extra zip in my step, so here is the chance."

Annette just laughed, "They will be some damn fools if they turn this down. Are we still meeting for drinks later?"

Shirley told her, "Yes, but I only have two hours to meet with you...Mama gotta go and get her freak on later on tonight." Annette asked, "Is it the same guy who came and saw me today?

Shirley told her "No, I have my personal boy toy and he is dying to see me."

Annette looked at her watch and realized the court session would begin shortly and she told Shirley she would call her when she was on her way to the bar. They hung up the phone and Shirley dialed another number.

The voice on the other end answered, "This is Mary Johnson." "Hey Mary, this is Shirley, just confirming your appointment for tomorrow morning."

Mary giggled and asked Shirley was she for real. "How am I going to recognize him? What are we going to do?"

Shirley told her "Don't worry about that, let me handle my business. All you have to do is don't say no, relax, and enjoy it, and believe me, you'll have that same glow that I have now."

Mary reminded Shirley she had been single for the last ten years, dating off and on, but could never find a winner out of the bunch.

Shirley told her "Stop looking for your knight in shining armor and just enjoy the ride."

Mary laughed and told her "I have nothing to lose. I look forward to this surprise which you have been promising me." And with that, Mary hung up the phone.

Shirley had one more call to make. As she dialed the number she could only smile as she found herself getting wet at the thought of hearing this man's voice. *Uumm*, she had to cross her legs over one another because all she could think about was his lips on her pussy.

<<*Ring. Ring. Ring.*>>

Shirley thought she was about to get voicemail until a man's voice answered.

"Hello!"

"How are you doing sexy lady?"

Shirley responded back and asked Willie how his day was going. He told her just fine but it would be better when he saw her later tonight. Shirley smiled and told him 'fine, I'll see you around 10:30 pm. Willie said no problem and hung the up phone. Shirley sat back in her office chair and daydreamed about the first time she and Willie actually made love. She remembered it was the fourth of July. Shirley's daydreaming was interrupted when the receptionist buzzed her on the telephone. She informed Shirley that Tyrone was here to see her.

Shirley had to readjust herself because she was soaking wet right now. Tyrone entered the office. He looked at Shirley and licked his lips. Even though Annette had been good, she was no way near the lover

that Shirley was. He thanked her again for the job and all the side hustling she was helping him with. He then asked for his next assignment and Shirley handed him an envelope. In the envelope was a picture of Mary and directions to where she would be tomorrow morning.

Tyrone smiled at Shirley and told her "At least none of your girls are ugly. I would have to charge you double then."

Shirley smiled at him and told him to always remember that the company you keep makes you who you really are. She continued explaining to him about Mary and her non-dating situation. She told him this assignment would be his toughest.

Tyrone told her "Don't worry, I'll take care of this." Shirley told him, "The same rules apply. If she says no or stops you in any way, do not give her the second envelope and just leave." She handed Tyrone a third envelope. He looked inside and saw the same $1,500 he had received for Annette. He smiled at Shirley, gave her a wink, and walked out the door.

Later that evening Shirley and Annette got

together for Happy Hour. Annette beat Shirley to the bar and had already ordered her second drink. When Shirley sat down, she discovered Annette had ordered her favorite drink. The drink was called a *'Fizzing Sherry'* and as Shirley took her first sip, Annette explained about what happened earlier that afternoon.

Annette told her "I knew I recognized that guy from your office, but I had no idea that he would be the one to come see me."

The only thing Shirley could do was pick up her glass. She made a toast and throughout the night the two ladies exchanged stories about Tyrone and all of his special abilities. Annette asked Shirley what other members she had in mind but Shirley told her to be patient and she would take care of the rest. Shirley laughed as she told Annette she was working on a stable of hot studs to satisfy the members of the Cougar Club.

Annette tried to keep her laughter low. Annette told her that if they were anything like the first guy then everything would be fine with her. The two talked and laughed over the next hour. Shirley then looked at her watch and realized she had to leave because she had a special night planned for her little boy toy. Annette tried to get her friend to stay but Shirley insisted she had to go, and with that, Annette was sitting at the bar by herself.

Shirley raced home and the thoughts of what she had planned made her hot. She was already horny because of what Annette got earlier that day and now it was time for her to have that same smile on her face.

Once at her house, Shirley began to lay out

her master plan for the evening. She looked around the tray she had set aside. Chocolate syrup, butterscotch sundae topping, a bowl of cut up fresh fruit that included bananas, oranges, and pineapples were on the tray. She also had a can of whipped cream. Shirley then placed eight of her silk scarves on her bed. She smiled thinking to herself; he has no idea what I have planned tonight. Shirley went to the bathroom to prepare the other surprise she had planned. She had a bag of red, yellow, and white rose petals.

She dialed Willie's cell phone number and she asked him if he was on his way. He told her he was about five minutes away and Shirley grew more excited eagerly anticipating what the night had to offer.

A familiar knock sounded on the door and as Shirley opened the door she realized that it had been too long since they had last seen each other. She gave Willie a hug and a kiss. After the hug and the kiss Shirley sat Willie down and she placed one of her silk scarves over his eyes. She asked him could he see and he told her no. Shirley led Willie into the bedroom and took off his clothes piece by piece. Once he was naked, Shirley led Willie over to her bathtub and she helped Willie into the very hot tub.

While leaning over the tub Shirley slowly began to give Willie a bath. She washed his entire body from head
to toe, his neck and ears, his chest and back, and as she was making her way to down to his dick and balls, she found him to be standing totally erect. This made Shirley hot with anticipation. With her soapy towel, she began to gently massage his balls. She even decided to play with Willie's dick, stroking it up and down, up and down. She didn't want Willie to

have an orgasm, so she stopped. She helped Willie out of the bathtub. Once again staring at his body, she had found her love goddess. Shirley slowly started to lick the water that was on Willie's body, it was as if Willie had some kind of control over her.

Shirley then grabbed a towel and took Willie to her bedroom. She helped him on top of the bed and slowly began to use the silk scarves she had pulled out. Once Willie was tied up good, Shirley took off his blindfolds and there she was standing in front of him wearing a
sexy nurse outfit. Willie knew he never could anticipate what Shirley was going to do.

Willie looked at her from head to toe; he became more excited because he couldn't touch her. Shirley began to place the fruit on Willie's body. She covered Willie's nipples with slices of bananas. Shirley placed several small pieces of banana on

Willie's chest and stomach.

Once she did this, she stood up and got off the bed, walked over to her stereo, and turned on some music. Shirley had arranged a mixture of music from jazz, some old Motown, and even some instrumental music. She picked up a feather that she had on her dresser, and slowly began to tease Willie around his feet. She slowly brushed the feather up his legs, played with his balls with it, went all around the bananas on his stomach and

chest, she even tickled his ears and neck with it.

Willie couldn't take the teasing that she was doing; he begged her to make love to him. He begged her to taste him, Shirley just smiled at him then she placed his dick into her mouth giving him oral pleasure that he wouldn't soon forget. She took her tongue and placed it at the base of his penis, slowly going up the shaft. She could see the veins in his penis pump more blood to keep his erection hard. She continued then went to play with his balls with her tongue gently massaging them. After doing this for several minutes, Shirley grabbed the chocolate syrup and began dripping it all over his body and she began to laugh.

Willie wanted her right now and she knew it. Shirley then began to eat the small pieces of banana while working her way up to his chest she licked every bit of

chocolate sauce off of him. This drove Willie crazy with anticipation. She bit the banana off his right nipple slowly licking the chocolate syrup while flicking her tongue around his nipple.

Willie told Shirley "just put me inside of you, I am about to cum."

Shirley refused. She bit the banana off the left nipple giving him the same pleasure while she played with his right nipple. She looked at Willie and asked him was he ready for her.

Willie's eye's rolled to the back of his head as he said "God, yes, please, please put me in your body!"

Shirley smiled at him and said "Your wish is my command."

Willie thought that his dick was going into Shirley's pussy but Miss Shirley had other plans. She climbed on

the bed and positioned herself so her pussy was right over Willie's face. She gently placed her pussy on his lips and his tongue immediately began to lick her. Willie was slurping and licking Shirley and she enjoyed every minute of it.

Shirley began to loudly moan, she began to move her hips in a circular motion. She was fucking Willie in his face with her pussy. Shirley pressed down harder as she let out an orgasm. She placed

Willie's dick into her mouth and slowly massaged her tongue up and down his penis. Shirley was having another orgasm and another. She loved the fact that this younger man could not eat enough of her pussy and it drove her crazy. She then turned around and positioned Willie's penis into her pussy. She told him she was going to try something different this time. She asked Willie if he wanted to try it with her.

Shirley then slid Willie's penis into her pussy but she didn't move back and forward, she didn't pounce on his dick, all she did was squeeze. Willie felt every muscle she had in her pussy. She looked Willie directly in his eyes and squeezed him again. She heard Willie's toes pop from excitement. He turned his head to the right enjoying the pleasure of what she was doing to him. Shirley then turned his head back and told him "Look at me!"

She continued to squeeze his penis with

great pleasure. She told Willie that she was going to squeeze an orgasm from his penis. Willie moaned with pleasure and Shirley continued to squeeze. Willie's moaning grew faster and faster and Shirley continued to squeeze. Willie then had an orgasm and Shirley continued to squeeze.

Willie was yelling "Oh shit…oh shit!! Damn!" and with that Willie shot a load into Miss Shirley. With Willie looking at her, never losing eye contact, Shirley then began to go backwards and forward on his penis. Now she was having an orgasm. Willie was bucking his hips trying to get every inch inside of Shirley. She felt a chill go over her body as her orgasm was released. She laid her head on his chest and softly squeezed his penis with her pussy. After laying there for several minutes Shirley reached up and freed Willie's hands. He wrapped his arms around her and held her tight as she looked up at him and they shared a kiss.

※

Across town, Annette sat on her sofa watching television and thinking about the events that had taken place earlier in the day. She became wet thinking how this perfect stranger had made her feel young again. She felt alive. She felt vibrant. Damn, she felt good.

She felt so good that she began touching herself again for the first time in years. She didn't even have to go upstairs and get her toy. She thought about the young man's mouth on her pussy and she slowly rubbed her clit. She only had a big t-shirt on so it was easy access. The more she thought, the more she rubbed and before she knew it she was having an orgasm.

Whew, she thought to herself, I should have done this a long time ago. I need to talk to Shirley and get some more action done. What the hell was I thinking by

skipping intimacy and sex for all these years? Annette then slowly laid her head on a pillow and drifted off to sleep with a big smile on her face.

MARY'S STORY

Mary Johnson

Mary is 45 years old and she is an executive vice president of a major sales company She is the first female to be Executive Vice President of a Fortune 500 company. She is a widow, her husband died about six years old. Mary has one daughter aged 18, who is a senior in high school.

Mary was busy putting together the conference of business executives. It was the showcase of the year with well over 200 companies participating. It seemed every year this conference grew bigger and bigger. This was its tenth year and Mary's fifth year of being in charge. Mary had no personal life outside of her business dealings. She had risen through the ranks as Vice President of Sales for her Fortune 500 company. She was always on point and was known as a strong business woman throughout her community and among her peers. She was fierce, yet polite. She was a hard charger, but humble. She was the total package and had no idea that her life was about to change and in such an orgasmic way.

Mary sat at a table where all the conference participants would sign in and get their credentials. One by one a who's who of the business elite came to her table. The event was all set up in a huge ballroom and she positioned herself to not only watch the door but to be able to see and hear all the speakers for that day. Once everyone had arrived Mary walked in, did her welcome, and turned the program over to a colleague. She then returned to her table and took a seat.

Tyrone entered the room and decked out in a very nice suit. Mary asked him, "Can I help you?"

Tyrone leaned over and told her "No, but I can help you."

Mary looked at him and again stated, "How can I help you sir?"

Tyrone licked his lips and told her "Shirley sent me".

Mary was shocked. Not at her conference. But damm, he looked good and he smelled even better. Tyrone sat down next to Mary. He asked her how long the program was and she told him they had about 30 minutes before the first break and about an hour or so before lunch.

Tyrone told her "That's all the time I'll need." Mary looked at him and said "So what happens next?"

Tyrone looked around to see if anyone was watching before he gently glided under the table. Mary's mouth opened wide. She thought what was he going to do here with all these people? Then someone walked in late to the conference. Mary had the late arrival sign in and as she was explaining the day's events to him, Tyrone slipped off her shoe and slowly began sucking

her toes. Mary felt a chill come over her body. She began to stutter her words and the guy asked her if she was okay. Tyrone was sucking her toes through her pantyhose and Mary was clearly turned on by this. He then gently moved a hand up her leg. As he moved his hand up her leg, Mary began to feel flush. She began to start sweating. The late registrant again asked her "are you sure you're okay?" Mary looked at him and said "hot flashes."

She then picked up her program and began fanning herself. Tyrone's hand had slowly made it up to her thighs and Mary opened eagerly to his hand. He began to rub her pussy and she felt herself getting wetter by the minute. Tyrone slid off Mary's other shoe and began sucking the toes on her other foot. Tyrone stopped sucking the toes and slid both hands up her skirt. Mary had no idea what going to happen next and quite frankly

she didn't give a damn. She felt Tyrone tugging at her pantyhose and panties. And she scooted up so he could slide them down. She could not believe the things she was doing but because she was so turned on, she couldn't stop now or she would be frustrated for the rest of the day.

Tyrone slowly pulled down the panty hose from Mary's legs, then her feet, he then caught a whiff of the sweet perfume she had put on. He sniffed the panty hose to take a deep breath of what Mary smelled like. Now he was rock hard He then moved his head up between Mary's legs and slowly began kissing her thighs and working his way back down to her feet. The room was spinning with pleasure for Mary. She felt herself getting wetter and wetter with every kiss. Tyrone continued to keep sucking on her toes. Mary could not believe what was going on under her table. Break time
was soon approaching and she was getting her freak on. After several more minutes of sucking on Mary's toes, Tyrone reached up and positioned himself to start licking her pussy.

Mary then slouched down further in her chair to give Tyrone full access. Tyrone began licking and sucking on Mary's pussy. Mary had an immediate orgasm but now she was really sweating. Tyrone loved the juices and the taste of Mary and he continued to lick her. Mary could not believe the feeling she was having. It had been a long time since a man touched that spot.

It was now break time and Mary found herself in a hard position. People were walking out smiling at her and Mary was having another orgasm. One guy who had a crush on Mary stopped by the table to chat for a moment. He was talking but Mary didn't understand a

word he was saying. Mary had to do something and do it fast. She was enjoying getting her pussy licked and this guy was about to ruin it. Mary leaned over and picked up her Blackberry. As she did this

Tyrone leaned with her and continued to lick her. Damn, she thought, a third orgasm?

The guy at the table asked Mary if she were okay. She looked at him and stated "hot flashes, can we talk later please?" He told her no problem. Mary continued to fan herself. She pulled out a handkerchief, dabbing her forehead and neck while Tyrone continued to eat her throughout the entire break.

One of Mary's assistants came to the table and asked about the short advertising scene they were about to show. She told the young lady to go in and start the film and that would be the cue for everyone to return to their seats so they could get started again. Tyrone never missed a beat. Mary continued to fan and Tyrone continued to eat. The lights went down and the short film started. The room was almost pitch dark except for the lights coming out of the projector. And when it happened--Tyrone stopped eating her and he looked from underneath the table and told her to come under the table with him.

Mary looked around and saw everyone was checking the film out. She disappeared underneath her table. She and Tyrone shared a kiss. Their tongues massaged each others as they both got lost in their own little world. Tyrone unzipped his pants and pulled out his dick. Mary positioned herself and Tyrone entered her body. She wanted to yell with pleasure as he continued to stroke her pussy. Tyrone was working it as fast and as hard as he could. Mary had another orgasm. Tyrone continued to stroke that pussy with everything he had and just as he was about to cum, Mary had a multiple orgasm. Tyrone shot his load deep into her pussy as they shared a deep kiss again.

Unexpectedly, it was at that moment that

someone came to Mary's table but since she wasn't there, they left her a quick note. Tyrone fixed his clothes and helped Mary slide her panty hose back on just before Mary realized he hadn't put her panties back on. Tyrone held them up with one hand and told her "You can have these, once we have our second meeting."

Mary smiled and tried to fix her hair. She knew the film was about to end. She peeked from underneath the tablecloth and with the coast clear, got up from underneath the table. Tyrone followed her shortly thereafter. As Mary walked out of the conference room to hurry to the bathroom, Tyrone handed her an envelope. Mary stuck the envelope in her pocket and Tyrone walked out the door. Mary entered the bathroom she had to hurry and wipe herself clean because she was still dripping wet with all of Tyrone's juices in addition to her own juices.

She could not believe how much fun and excitement she had just had. Mary then applied a panty liner to her pantyhose because she couldn't help thinking about Tyrone and that wonderful tongue of his. Mary straightened out her clothes, rechecked her hair, and thought about what she had just done. She could only smile to herself and say, "That damm Shirley, she is a fool! Lord, I got to thank her for that. Have mercy on me." After reapplying her lipstick Mary reached in her pocket. She pulled out the envelope Tyrone had given her. She then read the card which stated

---

"Welcome to the Cougar Club.

Give me a call later.

Shirley

Mary also noticed Tyrone had left his cell phone number. She smiled and walked back into the conference room just as the film was ending. Well this is the best conference ever known to man.

⁂

Later on that day Shirley telephoned Annette and Mary in a three-way call and invited them to dinner. She explained to them they were going to meet three or four new recruits.

Mary told Shirley "If they get half of what I got, then they will be fools to say no!"

Annette chimed in, "All I can say is anyone who isn't a card carrying member, she is a fool. I have had the best experience of my life and I just got started."

Shirley reminded Mary and Annette, "We can't give out too many hints at the dinner. They have to make this choice on their own free will. No longer will we sit on the sidelines and not be satisfied. I don't have to tell the two of you what a younger man can do for you. The pleasures that he will give you are nothing like we receive from these tired old men. And let's not forget the glow you will have hours upon hours once he leaves."

Both ladies said "yes" with grins on their faces.

"So--dinner is set tonight, 8:30 pm at my place, you can show up a bit early. So that way we can all talk without having someone eavesdrop on us."

"Are there any questions, ladies?"

Both Annette and Mary replied no and the call ended. Shirley flipped through her cell phone numbers and she had a similar conversation with several ladies. She pulled out her notepad and wrote down the following names:

Sheila Williams, tax accountant

Laverne Jackson, owner of an IT company

Janice Washington, RN

Bernice Potts, chief of police with DeKalb County

Andrea Smith, Assistant DA

Stephanie Brown, dentist

Shirley looked over the list of names for possible inductees into the Cougar Club. These ladies all had similar things in common. They were either divorced or widowed, kids were about to leave high school or already in college, and they were all upstanding citizens in their own communities but none of them had a man at the time. Shirley dialed one more number to check on the food she had ordered for tonight's dinner. The caterer told her everything was fine and Shirley and hung up the phone.

൞

Later that evening Annette and Mary arrived at Shirley's house around 8:15 pm. As they walked up to the door, another lady pulled up in her car. Annette recognized the lady and the ladies all shared a quick hug and Annette did the introductions.

"Mary, this is Andrea Smith, and she is an assistant district attorney. Mary works for one of the biggest sales companies in Atlanta."

Annette rang the doorbell. Shirley opened the door and welcomed in her guests. Shirley was sipping on a glass of wine and invited the ladies to her den. The ladies all sat down and started talking. The doorbell rang again. This time Sheila and Janice had arrived. As Shirley invited them in, Bernice was driving up and Shirley waited for her to get to the door. While waiting for Bernice, Shirley realized only one other lady was missing - Miss Stephanie Brown – who was Shirley's personal dentist. Just as Shirley closed the door, she heard Stephanie pull up. She once again stood at the door and waited for her.

Stephanie walked up, gave Shirley a hug, and joked about the traffic. Shirley laughed because Stephanie lived only six blocks from her. Shirley closed her front door and leaned against it. Taking another sip of her wine, she listened to the ladies talk. She enjoyed how the ladies were getting along and felt this was a great start to her new social club.

Shirley joined the ladies and the group talked for around an hour about everything from politics to the economy to dating. As the ladies ate their food and drank several bottles of wine, Shirley looked at Annette and Mary and winked at both of them and told them it was time. The other ladies looked around trying to figure out what was going to happen. Shirley stood in front of the room with Annette and Mary on her side. She began to explain what they were doing there. She continued as she explained about the Cougar Club and how she had formed the group because she was tired of ladies who were beautiful and educated but lonely and horny. One of the ladies shouted "I hear ya girl!"

Shirley went further and told the ladies about the initiation but didn't give them all the details. She told them Annette and Mary both had already been through the initiation, and then she pointed out the smiles on their faces and asked the ladies how many of them would like to have that same smile.

All of the ladies raised hands and a few second later Shirley raised her glass and stated "A toast to you all, and hopefully, the word 'no' will not come out of your mouths and I will see you all here again at our next meeting as members. Annette said 'Here. Here," and the ladies touched their glasses together and drank some more of their wine. The ladies began to mingle again. The new invitees were asking Annette and Mary all types of questions. The laughter and the questions continued for about another hour and slowly all the ladies left Shirley's house.

As Mary got into her car, she was still feeling horny from her earlier adventure with Tyrone. She couldn't invite him over to her house for a wild night of sex because her daughter was there so she called Tyrone and he eagerly agreed to meet her at a hotel in downtown Atlanta. After saying yes, Tyrone told her he would see her in about an hour. Mary smiled as the phone call ended. She called home to check on her daughter. Once Mary knew her daughter was situated, she headed to the hotel to wait for Tyrone.

Shortly thereafter, Mary pulled in to the Ritz Carlton. She pulled her car up to the front and the valet took her car. She went to the front counter and asked for a room. The lady at the registration desk asked how many nights would she be staying. Mary told her one night. The lady handed her a registration card and told her it would be $268 per night plus taxes. Mary pulled out her American Express card and handed it to the clerk. As she finished filling out the registration card, the clerk handed her a scan card and told her she would be on the 20th floor. She gave her the room number and a brochure explaining the Fitness Center, the restaurant, and several other amenities. Mary smiled at the lady, signed her credit card slip and walked towards the elevator to go to her room. Once she was inside the elevator, Mary texted Tyrone the information about the room and smiled again waiting for the elevator to reach her floor.

When Mary reached her floor, she opened the door to her room. She slowly began to take off her clothes. As she was undressing Mary walked into the bathroom and began filling up the tub with water for a nice hot bubble bath. She finished taking off her last piece of clothing and she slowly stepped into the bath. She had to remember to pull her hair up so it wouldn't get wet. After she pinned her hair, she sat down in the bathtub. The hot water and the bubbles felt so wonderful to her. She sat there in silence thinking about Tyrone and what he had done to her at the conference earlier that day.

Her nipples grew harder the more she thought about it. She couldn't believe it had been four years since someone had turned her on as much as her deceased husband. While Mary enjoyed her bath, and reminisced about Tyrone her fingers were slowly bringing her to an orgasm. This was something she hadn't experienced in years and she was enjoying this new sexual freedom. It was an unexpected pleasure and she couldn't wait to

unleash her desires on Tyrone.

Tyrone was making his way through the light traffic in downtown Atlanta. For some reason, Mary had touched a part of him and he felt himself wanting to be with her again. He loved this new gig that Shirley had lined up for him and deep down inside he figured his life was a lot better with his new set of friends. About twenty minutes later, Tyrone pulled up to the hotel. As he exited his car, he sent Mary a text saying "I'm on my way up."

Mary had finished her bath and was applying lotion to her body. She had all the tools she needed because she had planned this night earlier in the day. If Tyrone had said no she would have just gone home after Shirley's dinner. She had a surprise for him, one that he would never forget.

A few seconds later there was a knock at her hotel door. She looked through the peephole and there he was. She swung open the door, her hand on her hip and her robe opened wide, showing her matching bra and panty set.

Tyrone walked in and she told him "Now we are on an even playing field. You look nice but you won't need those clothes."

As Tyrone walked into the room, he took off his overcoat. Mary walked behind him, wrapping her arms around his waist. She whispered into his ear "Do you realize how you made me feel earlier today?"

While rubbing her hands over his chest and stomach, she turned him around and started to unbutton his shirt and as she finished the last button on his shirt, Tyrone took it off, and Mary lifted his t-shirt and pulled

it over his head. She kissed his right nipple then his left. Tyrone closed his eyes as the pleasure of her touching him drove him crazy. Mary reached for his belt and with one clean motion, unfastened it and pulled it away from his pants. Tyrone stepped out of his shoes and Mary walked over to the bed and pulled the sheets back.

As he looked at Mary, he noticed everything about her from how smooth her skin looked to her matching bra and panty set. He noticed how nice her pedicure was; he even loved the texture of her hair. Earlier in the day, he didn't have time to pay attention to these things, and savor them, so now, every second that he looked at her, he became hornier. She was truly a beauty and she had sex written all over her face. He couldn't wait to please her.

Mary dropped the robe to the floor, took off the pumps she was wearing and climbed into bed. She patted her hand on the bed inviting Tyrone to join her. After he slid his pants off, he obliged her. Their lips were on a one-way track and they slowly kissed each other. Tyrone ran his hands over Mary's back and buttocks and Mary did the same. He began to kiss her neck and massage her breasts. Mary was turned on even more. As Tyrone's lips slowly made their way to her breasts, he was feeling for her bra fastener but couldn't find it. Mary chuckled and unfastened her bra from the front, exposing her breasts to this younger man that she could just eat alive.

He was so charming and handsome yet slow and careful in how he treated her body. Tyrone sucked on her breasts nice and slow massaging her nipples with his

tongue. He then made his way down to her stomach and slowly made circle motions around her belly button. He positioned himself to lick Mary's pussy. This time he enjoyed it twice as much. She was clean-shaven and Tyrone tried to eat as much of her pussy as he could. Mary moaned with pleasure. This time was better than earlier today. She opened her legs wider to allow him to dig his tongue in deeper. And as he did, she had an orgasm. She grabbed the back of his head and the orgasm became more intense. Tyrone continued to lick her body and Mary enjoyed every minute of it. She pulled Tyrone up and told him she had a surprise for him.

She told Tyrone in a joking manner "...and you can't say no," and then she told him to lie on his back.

She pulled out a bag of treats she had hidden underneath the bed. Mary told Tyrone to close his eyes to get ready for his surprise. As he did, his mind was racing. He had no idea what she had planned for him. This was new to him. His ex-wife did not like to try a lot of freaky things. He had done more freaky things with these women than ever with his wife. He couldn't wait to see what she had in store for him, plus he thought it was cute how she said he couldn't say no. He had no intentions of ever saying no to her.

Mary climbed back on top of him, except this time, she put him in a 69-position and softly put her pussy on his face. Tyrone began to lick her body and enjoy the taste of her pussy all over again. As he licked her body, he wrapped his hands around her waist and began to devour her pussy even more.

Mary pulled out a row of beads and as she was trying to remain focused, she lubricated them. Once she did, she put Tyrone's penis into her mouth attempting to swallow the whole thing. As she did this, she positioned the beads right at Tyrone's ass. He could feel the lubrication and wondered what she was doing.

She took his dick out of her mouth and told him "Relax and breathe, trust me, you will enjoy this."

As she rubbed her pussy more into his face, Tyrone relaxed and Mary began inserting the beads into his ass. One by one she put the beads into his ass until she was at number six. She then continued to suck his dick and play with his balls. Tyrone could feel the beads in his ass and it was actually turning him on. The more Mary sucked, the more he squeezed his ass, the hotter it made him. As Tyrone began to have an orgasm, Mary pulled one bead out of his ass. It made his dick harder as he

gently stroked his g-spot. He had no idea why this was turning him on. He had heard stories about this but he

had never experienced it. His ex-wife never would attempt anything as freaky as this. This was something he wouldn't have attempted either. He began to moan louder and Mary knew that he was about to have an orgasm. She pulled another bead out of his ass. This made his dick rock hard and it began to throb and jump. Tyrone was on the verge of a major orgasm like he had never had before. As he began his orgasm, Mary pulled another bead out of his ass. She began to swallow his juices as she pulled another bead out of his ass. Tyrone's yells were muffled because he had a mouth full of pussy and Mary enjoyed every minute of it.

As he began to shoot more of his juices into her mouth, Mary began to have an orgasm and pulled another bead out of Tyrone's ass. Tyrone again was yelling as loud as he could and yelling as Mary pulled the last bead out of his ass. He was still coming and had never cum so hard in his life before. She was turning him out and he loved it.

Mary then turned around and placed Tyrone's penis into her pussy. She moaned then he moaned even louder because his dick was very sensitive at that moment. Mary was galloping on his dick and grinding her pussy as Tyrone began to have another orgasm. Mary reached back with one of her hands and began to play with his balls. He was moaning and yelling so loud that she had to put her hand over his mouth.

She looked at him, smiled, and said "Now you see how you made me feel earlier today" as she slowly grinded Tyrone's dick.

Mary wanted to make sure she had every drop of his love juices. He removed her hand from his mouth. She bit his lower lip and with a sucking motion she kissed him and pulled the air out of his body.

Once Tyrone was finished, Mary just stayed on top of him, looked into his eyes and said "Thank you for awakening both me and my body."

"No, thank you. You taught me something tonight!" said Tyrone.

Mary had worn Tyrone out and he drifted off to sleep. Mary soon followed...sleeping like a big baby.

Laverne's Story

Laverne Jackson

Laverne is 44 years old. She is the owner of an IT company. Prior to opening her own company, she worked for the Federal government and designed a web database for the Department of Defense. She has no children. She has been divorced for six years.

It was Sunday morning and Laverne was up and preparing to go to church. She couldn't wait to hear the word the pastor had to give today. This was the one place she felt total serenity. If only she knew this would be the best church experience of her young life. She made one quick check in the mirror, applied her lipstick, and walked out the door. Laverne drove down the road, turning to her favorite Gospel station and putting herself in the mood for Praise and Worship. She soon pulled into the church parking lot. The parking lot was packed. She grabbed her Bible and exited her car. She walked up to the church and was greeted by others as she greeted new people as well.

She took her position as an usher, grabbed a stack of offering envelopes, and stood her post. Scanning the congregation, she looked over and saw

Shirley and waved at her friend, and then she clapped as the Senior Choir sang their last song before the preacher stood up to give the word. The senior choir began to sing Marvin Sapp's *Never Would Have Made It,"* and as the choir was halfway through the song, Shirley looked at Tyrone and gave him a wink.

Tyrone stood up and walked over to Laverne. He asked her could he speak to her for a moment. Laverne didn't want to leave because she wanted to hear the end of the song. Laverne stepped outside the sanctuary into another part of the church. Tyrone was following her.

He whispered and told her "Shirley sent me." Once she heard the words, Laverne's jaw opened wide. The only words she could get out were "Say that again?"

Tyrone repeated, "Shirley sent me".

Laverne was stuck between a rock and a hard

place. She knew if she said no she would never get a second chance. She looked at Tyrone and asked "Are you serious?"

He told her "Yes. Very."

Tyrone grabbed her hand and pulled her into a room and closed the door behind him. The only thing Laverne kept saying was "Are you serious? Right here at the church?"

Tyrone then placed a finger over Laverne's lips and she closed her eyes. He began to kiss her on her neck. She felt goosebumps all over her body. Tyrone began to nibble on Laverne's ear and Laverne dropped every offering envelope in her hand. The choir had stopped singing and the pastor was standing before the congregation. Tyrone sat Laverne down on some steps
in the room they were in and Laverne realized she was sitting on the stairs for the baptismal pool

which was located directly behind the area where the pastor was

preaching. All of a sudden it didn't matter where they were, she was ready.

He got down on his knees and slowly began kissing her feet and working his way up her legs. Tyrone began to nibble on her thighs. He slowly began to move towards her pussy and the only thoughts that came to Laverne's mind were "No, not here in the church, I am going straight to Hell but damn, that feels so good." She then began to stroke the back of Tyrone's head as he slowly made his way to her panties. He pulled her panties to the side and began to lick her pussy. Laverne began to shake with great pleasure and excitement.

The pastor was deep into his sermon now and they could clearly hear him preaching. He was talking about not being ashamed of saying "Hallelujah" and "Amen" and so he asked the congregation to give him an *"Amen"*. Laverne was having an orgasm at that moment and she shouted out *"Amen!"* The pastor heard a voice coming from behind him and was a little stunned. He asked the church for a *Hallelujah* and Laverne was still cumming and she sang out *"Oh HALLL-LE-LU-JAH!!!"* The pastor heard another Hallelujah from behind him and again he was stunned; he told the church "I'm hearing the echoes but I don't feel like you mean it!"

Tyrone was still licking Laverne and then he positioned himself and began to unzip his pants. He pulled out his penis at the same time the pastor shouted, "Give me an Amen." Tyrone turned Laverne over and had her right leg two steps higher than her left leg. Tyrone thrust his entire penis deep into Laverne's pussy. The pastor asked for another *"Amen"* and Laverne yelled out *"AMEN....A-MEN!!!"* The pastor once again heard the echoes of an Amen coming from behind him and told the church, if you believe a miracle is coming and your blessing is coming right here today, if you feel a release, can I get a "Hallelujah."

At the same time Tyrone was pumping every inch of his penis into Laverne. He went deeper than any man had ever gone into her before. And Laverne yelled out "HALLLLLEE LU JAH, HALLLE LU JAH …Oh HALLELUJAH…with Laverne having her fifth orgasm of the morning, Tyrone had one himself. And as he was coming, he began to grunt loudly and he leaned his head against the center of Laverne's back and was screaming and moaning. After he was done with his orgasm, he wrapped his arms around Laverne and he had every inch of himself inside her. He was shaking from coming so hard he pulled out of Laverne's pussy. They looked into each other's eyes and shared a kiss. Both Laverne and

Tyrone had sweat popping off their foreheads.

She showed him where the bathroom was so he could clean up and she needed to clean up as well. As Laverne walked to the bathroom, she could feel her panties were soaking wet. She had to take her panties off or she would have to wear wet panties throughout the rest of the service. Laverne decided that after she cleaned up, she would go back and get her offering cards and go back in through the main entrance of the church. Once Tyrone was cleaned up, he handed Laverne an envelope and he left the church. Laverne sat through another 20 minutes of church and couldn't get her mind off of Tyrone. After the service was over with, Laverne made a straight line over to Shirley.

As she hugged her, she whispered in her ear, "Girl, I knew you were a freak, but to send him to me at CHURCH?"

Shirley just whispered back "You never know when I'm gonna get ya...that's the whole point of the Cougar Club. We now live our lives spontaneously. We never take no for an answer and we always get what we want."

Laverne pulled out the envelope that Tyrone had given her and saw the note from Shirley. It read:

'Never thought I would have gotten you here, huh? Ha-ha Ha-ha,

Welcome to the Cougar Club.

Shirley

P.S. You know you enjoyed it!

Laverne looked at Shirley and told her "One day, I'll get you back for this one." Laverne drove home with a big smile on her face. She hadn't felt this alive in years. Tyrone brought something out of her today. She was sure she would never go back to boring old sex with pill toting men. She thought to herself her experience at church gave new meaning to the pastor's word *'release'*.

Sheila's Story

Sheila Williams

Sheila is a professional tax accountant and owns her own firm with offices in two states — Georgia and North Carolina. She is 47 years old, has 2 kids — 21 and 19, who are both in college, She is divorced and hasn't had a relationship in about four years.

Sheila Williams

It was Monday morning and Sheila had arrived at her office early to prepare for her staff meeting and make sure all of her clients were being taken care of properly. Sheila had 14 supervisors and over 125 staff spread out over two different states. Sheila's life had become her company's life. She drank, ate, and slept the United States Tax Code twelve months of the year; she was always busy helping everyone else keep their businesses organized and running smoothly.

Shelia was excited because she had opportunity to handle Shirley's company and she was ecstatic about the new addition. She was sitting in her office, phone lines were ringing, and people were walking and forth all the time. One of her supervisors came to her office and told

her about a problem in the Charlotte office. Shelia

didn't have to travel to the office but set up an emergency phone conference with the staff there. About this time, she got a text message from Shirley and it said "Are you ready?"

She didn't return the text right away. About five minutes later, Tyrone walked into her office. When the receptionist buzzed and told Sheila she had a visitor, she asked the receptionist who it was. Tyrone told the receptionist just let her know Shirley had sent him." The receptionist relayed the message and Tyrone walked into the office. He walked over to Sheila and told her again, "Shirley sent me." Sheila told him, "Wait a second; I've got to finish something." Tyrone walked over towards her and began to rub her shoulders. He began to give her shoulders a massage, Sheila slumped back in her chair. The massage felt so good to her. He was making her forget about her work. Tyrone told her she was too

tense for it to be so early in the morning. He then began to kiss her on the neck and she felt herself get all excited. Shelia started moaning "Ooh, oooh yes!" At that moment her receptionist buzzed in again and told her the Charlotte conference call was all set up and ready to go.

Shelia jumped out of her chair, told Tyrone "Baby, you sure look good today, but I got to go to work right now." Tyrone pulled Sheila closer to him. He attempted to kiss her but she pushed him and said "Sweetie, not right now. Can you come to my house later tonight?"

He said "No, that's not possible, please talk to Shirley." Tyrone walked out of her office. And when she thought about it, she hurried out of the office behind him and told him to wait.

"Can you give me about an hour? Can you have a

seat in my office and I'll be done in an hour," she explained to Tyrone.

He stopped and turned around and told her "No, you need to call Shirley," and with that, he walked out the door and left Sheila's building.

Once he returned to his car, Tyrone called Shirley and gave her the news. She knew that with him calling so early, the visit had not turned out good. The rest of the day Sheila sat at her desk and trying to figure out a way to ask Shirley for a second chance to join the social club. Her 15 minute conference call to her Charlotte office had cost her a chance to join Shirley's elite social club. She knew she could have postponed the conference call because she was in charge of her company. Once again, she let her company dictate how her life was being lived and now she was regretting that wrong decision she made today. She finally picked up her Blackberry and texted Shirley to explain what had happened. Her message was two pages long. She received Shirley's response and it was very plain with only five letters. *S-O-R-R-Y*

Janice's Story

Janice Washington

Janice is 43 years old. She has a Master's in Nursing and she is the Director of Nursing at a large hospital in downtown Atlanta. She has one son who is 17.

Janice Washington

It was Monday night and Janice had just arrived at the hospital to begin her shift. She'd had a great weekend with friends and was even more excited about the telephone call she received from Shirley telling her that she had a surprise waiting for her at the hospital. Janice had no idea when or where her gift would be given and she didn't care. If it meant that she would have the glow and smile like Shirley, she was ready. Janice looked at the clock and realized it was 3:30 in the morning and time for her lunch break. She walked to the elevator to go to the café downstairs to grab a salad when she was pulled into the linen closet by Tyrone. When Tyrone told her "Shirley sent me," Janice grew hot and wet at the same time. She asked him to repeat what he said but he didn't, instead, he kissed her and she loved it.

He began rubbing her breasts and he could tell she was turned on. Janice started moaning. Damn she could understand why Shirley had that glow. Tyrone was kissing her on her neck and then he nibbled on her ear, Janice was getting wetter by the minute. He lifted up her shirt and started kissing her chest, he removed her bra and he began sucking her breasts. He nibbled her nipples and Janice felt as if she was about to have an orgasm, this man was taking her and not taking no for an answer. He began to kiss and suck on her other breast. When he then got on his knees and began to take her pants off, Janice was more than willing to take it all off for this younger man. Damn, Janice thought to herself, if this is what Shirley was getting no wonder she is happy as hell!

Once her pants and thong were off, Tyrone began to eat her pussy. He was licking her pussy lips and then he stuck his tongue in her pussy. Janice was about to yell with pleasure as she began to have an orgasm right in his mouth. She grabbed a towel and pushed her face into it and yelled softly. Tyrone was still eating her and he wouldn't stop. Janice was having another orgasm. She was so used to pleasuring herself that she never tried and now she had two orgasms in one night for the first time in years. She looked down at the younger man eating her pussy and she had another orgasm.

He then stood to his feet and lifted Janice up in the air, she wrapped her legs around him and he slid her down on his penis…she moaned again from great pleasure as he opened up her pussy…she felt her pussy being stretched to its limit. Janice then had another

orgasm. He was bouncing her up and down on his dick. Tyrone was enjoying this pussy. Damn he was trying his best not to have an orgasm but this pussy was so good and wet. After fucking her in this position for five more minutes he let her down but kept her left leg up and began to long dick Janice. Janice had no complaints. She felt as though she was about to cum again and asked Tyrone if he would lick her some more, he got back on his knees and began licking her pussy. Janice enjoyed having his tongue in her pussy. Tyrone was licking her clit and massaging it with his tongue and Janice had another orgasm. She was rubbing the back of his head and pushed his face into her pussy as she had her orgasm this time.

Tyrone stood up and turned Janice around. She bent over and he tried to put his dick into her pussy but it was so wet it took several attempts. He moaned loudly as he got in and it felt so good. He grabbed her hair and

pulled it as he fucked her hard and fast. Tyrone

was about to cum. Janice was so turned on she had yet another orgasm and Tyrone shot a juicy load of semen into her pussy. Janice moaned with great pleasure. Tyrone pulled his penis out of her but she wanted more. He fixed his clothes and handed her an envelope from Shirley. Janice didn't give a damn about any envelope at this moment. She was still horny and wanted more. She looked at Tyrone and he told her he had to leave.

She could only smile and tell him "I will see you later."

Janice fixed her clothes and rushed to the bathroom to clean up. She was wet all over. Once she cleaned up and returned to her desk, the other nurses asked her what she did for lunch. She told them she had decided to work-out. Smiling, she opened the envelope. It read

"He is good, isn't he?

Welcome to the Cougar Club.

Shirley

Janice put everything in her pocket and all she could do was laugh at Shirley.

Bernice's Story

Bernice Potts

Bernice is 51 years old. She has been widowed for four years. Bernice is the first female chief of police for DeKalb County, Georgia, a suburb of Atlanta. She has a son who is 25 years old and he is an educator.

Bernice Potts

Bernice was an up and coming force to be dealt with in the law enforcement community. Her social life, however, was a horrible story. Most of the men she would try to date had a problem dealing with her because of her position plus a number of men were intimidated by her. She longed for a strong man who would take her in his arms and make her feel like the woman she was, but as always she found herself single and alone.

That was--until she met Shirley at a local event and the two quickly became friends. They would talk just about every day and Bernice would always burn her ear off about the glow that she had. Bernice wanted to

know the secret behind Shirley's glow. She knew it

was a man, but couldn't get Shirley to spill the story behind it. Shirley told Bernice she would share this secret one day and now that day had arrived. Bernice had finished her work for the day and she was rushing home from work to get ready for a fund raiser that evening for the District Attorney.

Bernice made it to her house and quickly jumped in the shower. Afterwards she rushed around getting dressed before heading downstairs to wait for her limo to pick her up for the event. She texted Shirley and asked her did she forget about her promise and Shirley texted back No! The limo arrived and Bernice opened the door and hopped in. She did not want to be late. A man was sitting in the limo and she asked "Who are you?"

It was Willie and he smiled and told her Shirley had
sent him. He pulled off her shoes and began

sucking on her toes. Bernice knew the rules emphasized she couldn't say no, besides this was feeling very good. She was glad she had gotten her toes done. Willie sucked her toes and took his time. Bernice felt her pussy getting wet and she was clearly turned on. She now understood why Shirley was smiling all the time. Damn, Bernice thought, he is sucking the hell out of my toes.

Willie moved up her legs and kissed them both softly going back and forth between them. He finally made his way up to her pussy when he softly pulled her panties and Bernice lifted her hips and he took them off, then he opened her legs and began to lick her pussy lips. Bernice laid her head back and enjoyed every lick he gave her. She couldn't believe Shirley would do this to her and in the limo at that. Willie was licking her pussy lips and even stabbing his tongue into her pussy. Bernice moaned and squeezed the hand rest in the car. She was having an orgasm. Damn this feels so good was the only thought she could come up with at the moment. She was grooving her hips into Willie's face and loving it. She was even more turned on by the fact that this younger man was eating her. Most of the men she tried to date would never eat her pussy and she would always be disappointed by this fact. Willie was having a wonderful time eating Bernice and she lifted her leg to give him more of her pussy to eat. This younger man was turning Bernice out with his eating skills. Before she knew it she had one leg resting on the door and the other up on the seat. She wanted her young Romeo to eat all he wanted, and with that she was having another orgasm.

Willie pushed in two of his fingers while he was still eating her. Bernice was coming again. Willie pulled out his penis and stuck it at the entry of

Bernice's pussy.

She couldn't take anymore as she realized she had more orgasms in this short limo ride than in the past month. Willie pushed his entire penis into her hot and wet pussy. Bernice moaned even louder because she was coming again and again…it had been so long since she had a dick move in and out of her like this….damn, damn, damn this dick was good to her…she didn't want to go to the event now…she wanted to continue fucking this young stallion. She was having more fun in the back of the limo than she would have during the evening smiling at fake ass folks at the fund-raising event.

Willie had now placed her legs up to the roof of the limo and he was banging Bernice with everything that he had and she was having another orgasm. Willie began to grunt and moan, this older woman had some of the best pussy he had since he fucked Shirley. Willie continued to pump as he was shooting his load deep into her pussy. He thought he was finished and sat back in his seat

when Bernice moved over to him and began sucking his dick. Willie was shocked, he had given her his best and she wanted more.

Bernice was sucking and playing with his dick with her tongue. Bernice thought, *oh well, fuck it…might as well have my fun as well,* as she took Willie's entire penis in her mouth. He began to moan and moan, damn, he was about to cum. He looked at Bernice and she smiled while she continued to suck and play with his balls. Willie's eyes began to roll to the back of his head. He began to cum and Bernice just continued to suck. She swallowed and licked his penis and she thanked him for a wonderful trip. The two had been so caught up in their own little world they didn't even realize the limo was pulling up to the event. Bernice asked the driver to circle around one more time. She had to clean up a little.

Willie handed her a bag with what she needed whispering "Shirley sent this to you." Bernice smiled and told him "Didn't think I would return the favor, huh?" Willie smiled and continued to try and catch his breath. Bernice saw an envelope with her name on it. She opened it and read it:

—

Hope you didn't drive my little sweetie too crazy!

I thought you might enjoy him.

Welcome to the Cougar Club.

       Shirley

PS: Call me after the event.

–

Bernice cleaned up and as she was ready to exit the limo, she told Willie "I will see you later, Baby," before she kissed him and got out of the limo. Willie could only sit

back and smile. Meanwhile across town Shirley got a text which read *"It's done, she is a wild cat."* Shirley smiled and continued to watch T.V

Andrea's Story

Andrea Smith

Andrea is 43 years old and she has been divorced for two years. She is a former police officer who attended law school at night to obtain her law degree. She is an Assistant District Attorney. She has a son 20 years old and he is in the United States Air Force.

A guilty verdict in her murder trial…Andrea had done it again. She was the hottest Assistant District Attorney in Atlanta. She was happy and wanted to celebrate but had no one special in her life to help her celebrate. She went back to her office, opened a bottle of juice and just relaxed. She kicked off her shoes and enjoyed the moment. Her feet were killing her, the shoes were cute but they did hurt after awhile. Suddenly, there was a knock on her door; little did she know it was a knock that would knock her socks off.

Andrea sang out "Come in…it's open."
In walked Tyrone, he looked at the beautiful woman and told her "Shirley sent me" and then he smiled.

Andrea didn't know what to do. She sat up in her desk and told him to come in. Grabbing her BlackBerry™ she turned it on and noticed Shirley had sent her a message. The message was her surprise was on the way. Andrea also knew her boss would be coming in soon.

Tyrone asked her if her feet hurt but before she had a chance to respond, he walked around her desk and gently took her foot and started rubbing it. Andrea closed her eyes; the foot rub was feeling sooooo good. Hell, she deserved this foot rub. What else would come with this she was wondering? Andrea decided to ask Tyrone, "So what else do I get?"

He looked at her and smiled…he knew she had no idea. After rubbing both of her feet, he moved to her shoulders and began rubbing them. Andrea was really enjoying this moment even more now. Tyrone began to

kiss her neck and he could hear her take a deep breath, he knew she was turned on now….there was no turning back.

He slowly started to kiss her ears and then moved to kiss her pretty lips. Andrea was so excited that she eagerly accepted his lips and tongue. The two shared a very passionate kiss. He slowly rubbed her breast and got on his knees and then he opened her legs and began to kiss her thighs. Andrea got so wet she felt her panties become soaked with her juices. He pulled her panties to the side and began licking her pussy. A knock on the door interrupted them. Tyrone crawled under her desk. Andrea tried to get her voice together before she answered "Come in."

It was the District Attorney. He was stopping by to offer congratulations on her biggest win to date. He sat on the edge of her desk and began talking. Tyrone started right back eating her pussy. Andrea was trying to

give him access without giving herself away. The

D.A continued to talk and Tyrone continued to eat. Andrea was in a bad spot. She was now having an orgasm right in her boss's presence. She could not believe it. She wanted to laugh but realized she would have to explain. The D.A told her a bad joke and it was her moment to let out some of her excitement. Andrea laughed at the joke.

She even began to wipe her forehead. She was breaking into a sweat trying not to moan as her young lover continued to eat her pussy. Andrea was laughing inside about how much hornier she was becoming having her pussy eaten while someone was sitting at her desk. Another co-worker came entered her office and now she was having another orgasm. Hell, Andrea was cool as long as she didn't yell out loud.

Tyrone had to keep from laughing as well. He knew he was driving her crazy and she couldn't do anything

about it. He began to stick his fingers in her pussy while he licked her. He was amazed at how wet she had become. She had juices flowing everywhere. Andrea was leaning back in her chair…giving her lover even more access. She was having the time of her life. Finally the two visitors left her office and she let out a sigh of relief. She had a total of four orgasms while they were in her office and even after they left, Tyrone was still eating and wouldn't stop. Andrea had thought he couldn't give her another orgasm, but Tyrone was not stopping.

He got from under the desk and sat her on top of it. He opened his pants and showed Andrea what he was about to give her. Her eyes looked at him with amazement. She was more than excited to try and handle this dick. Tyrone put himself in place and pushed his penis into her pussy. Andrea let out a moan. It had been so long since she had gotten her freak on, and now, here she was doing things she never thought of

herself doing. Tyrone was working it…in and out…in and out. Andrea had another orgasm. She was ready to pass out. She had taken enough.

She looked at Tyrone with a look of "I give up."

Tyrone smiled as he continued to nail that pussy as he began to pump harder and had his own orgasm. He pulled out and began to clean himself up. Andrea did the same. After a few minutes talking and cleaning up, Tyrone gave Andrea an envelope. She asked what it was and he told her everything she would need was inside. And with that -- he walked out the door. Andrea sat back at her desk and opened up the envelope. It was a note from Shirley which read:

Nothing makes a work day better than getting your freak on.

Welcome to the Cougar Club.

Shirley

Andrea smiled and thought to herself, *"That damn Shirley."* She then sent her a text message that read *"Girl, you are the bomb....glad we are friends, and I see why you are smiling every day.* Not only was Andrea the hottest DA in Atlanta, she was now the newest member of Cougar Club. She had more orgasms today than ever before and her sexual frustrations were completely satisfied.

Stephanie's Story

Stephanie Brown

Stephanie is 46 years old and she is a dentist. She has been divorced for three years. She has daughter, 22 years old, who was recently accepted into a dentistry program with the goal of following her mother in the world of dentistry

Stephanie Brown

It was Thursday evening and Shirley's Club was almost complete. She had amassed a great group of ladies to begin with. All were very professional women in their own respective fields. Shirley sent a text message to all the ladies telling them about the dinner at her place on Saturday evening. Once again, she welcomed them all to the Cougar Club.

A few minutes later Shirley received a text from Stephanie. The message said *"we have to talk. I have not done my initiation yet"*. Shirley dialed Stephanie's number and Stephanie answered. Shirley told her that she had not forgotten about her and by the time the meeting started she would be in the club. Stephanie just smiled

and laughed, saying "Okay, how ever you want to do it." The two talked a few minutes more and then hung up the phone.. All day Friday Stephanie wondered what time her initiation was going to take place.

First came lunchtime. Lunchtime arrived and no initiation. She closed her dentist's office around 5:00 pm. It was now 9:00 pm and still no initiation. Stephanie began to wonder if she had been put out the club before she ever got in it? Stephanie arrived home and poured a glass of wine. She sat on her sofa and turned on the television. The entire time she wondered what was her initiation? What would she have to do? Before long, Stephanie drifted off to sleep and when she awakened, she initially panicked. She texted Shirley a message and explained to her how she had fallen asleep. Shirley sent her back a message and told her she was good but she also warned her *'Be prepared and don't say no. I will see you later this evening. Have a wonderful day.'*

Stephanie decided to text one of the ladies she knew from the meeting and told her she was looking forward to seeing her at the meeting in the evening. Sheila sent Stephanie a text reply where she tried to explain how crazy this past week had been and how she had said "No" to Shirley's surprise. Stephanie tried to get information from Sheila about the process, and even though Sheila had said no, she wasn't about to explain to her what would happen.

Later that evening, Stephanie arrived at Shirley's house and when Shirley opened the door, Stephanie asked Shirley what was going on? Shirley asked her to come inside and have a seat and told her she would explain everything to her later.

While walking into Shirley's home, a man approached

Stephanie and said to her "Shirley sent me."

Stephanie was so excited and happy to finally find out what made Shirley glow and have such a wonderful smile. The man escorted Stephanie into another room and then into a closet. He told her his name was Tyrone. He then spun her around and began to kiss her on the back of her neck. Stephanie had goosebumps all over her body. She was excited to have the touch of a man for the first time in a long time. Tyrone continued to kiss Stephanie on her shoulders and then on her neck and finally on her ears. He began to unfasten her pants and slowly slid the pants down to her ankles and revealed the black lace thong she was wearing. He got on his knees and slowly began to kiss her legs. Each kiss became more sensual to Stephanie. She was already in another world.

Tyrone then pulled down her thong and asked

her to step out of it. Tyrone began to kiss her inner thighs and finally made his way to her pussy. She was already dripping with her juices. As he played with her pussy lips with his tongue her legs began to shake. He flicked his tongue over and around her clit and she had an orgasm. He continued to lick her pussy and she continued to have orgasms. For Stephanie, it was like one very long orgasm. For Tyrone, it felt as if he put his face into a sink full of water. The more he licked, the wetter she became. Stephanie lifted her leg and positioned it on a nearby shoe rack. She was inviting his tongue to go deeper in her pussy and she wanted to put her juices all over his face.

Tyrone stood up and unzipped his pants. He moved Stephanie's hands down to his penis and asked her to take it out. Stephanie obliged him and when she saw his penis, the only thing she could think was *'Where are you going to stick that?'* Her pussy had only been stroked with her Bullet™ for the past two years. Tyrone positioned himself to enter her body, Stephanie gazed directly in his eyes and asked him to be gentle. Inch by inch Tyrone worked his penis into her very tight pussy. The more he worked at it, the more her juices came. Tyrone slowly began to pump his penis in and out of her pussy.

Stephanie began to have another orgasm. She wrapped her arms around him and was pleading with him to give her more. Now her juices were running down his leg. This turned both of them on even more. Tyrone began

to grunt and to moan and before he knew it he was having his own orgasm. Once he finished, the two shared a quick kiss and Stephanie just smiled at him. He pulled out an envelope and handed it to her before he left the closet. As Stephanie left the closet, she hurried to one of Shirley's bathrooms. She cleaned herself up and opened the envelope which Tyrone had given her.

—

You are as beautiful in the dark as you are in the light.

    Welcome to the Cougar Club!

                          Shirley

—

After getting herself pulled together, Stephanie walked into the den where all the ladies were sitting. Shirley made an announcement:"Now that our last initiation has taken place, I would like to thank you all as well as welcome you to the Cougar Club. But before we go any further, let me introduce you to the two gentlemen whom you already know. "Ladies, say hello, and welcome to the Cougar Club's two newest boy toys Tyrone who is 35 and Willie who is 34. I am sure we all had a wonderful experience with them, right...."

The ladies began to mumble amongst themselves, smiling and giggling, as they waved to the two men. Bernice looked at Shirley and asked her whether she was joking about their ages.

Shirley laughed and said "No, that's the whole point of the Cougar Club. We will no longer settle for the men our age and older waiting for a blue pill to take effect and then not be satisfied. We are doing the same things that men our ages are doing and have been doing for years. The older men date younger women and so we're going to fuck younger men. These two gentlemen love to date and sleep with older women so we will have all our fun and be satisfied and they won't complain at all.

"I am sad to report that one of my original members did not make the cut. I warned you all not to say no but she did anyway. But this was something I wanted to do for some of my girlfriends to make sure we are all satisfied."

Mary raised a question. She wanted to know how would they all share just two men? Shirley told her that she had some other new recruits coming and she would reveal them soon. She explained the new guys as well as

Tyrone and Willie would be accompanying them on a Caribbean vacation. The ladies began to chatter amongst themselves again exchanging stories about the two men.

Shirley announced dinner was served, but before they went to the dining room she had something for each of them. One by one Shirley gave each lady a pin. The pin had the same symbol as the insignia on the card they had received at their initiation. Each lady placed her pin on her blouse, smiling as she remembered the pleasure she had received. Later they sat at the table and laughed and joked about their initiations. All the ladies agreed that it was a tie between Laverne's initiation and Andrea's and they couldn't agree on which one was more freaky or intense. The ladies laughed and then it hit them, they wanted to know how Shirley got initiated. She sat down, a glass of wine in her hand and took a sip, then she smiled, looking around the room at

all her ladies, and started to tell them the story, but she stopped, and decided to let Willie tell the story. Willie came over to the coffee table. He sat down and taking a sip of his wine, he asked them "Have you ever seen someone and wanted them with all your life, with every bit of air in your body?"

"Have you ever seen someone and wanted them more than anything else in your life? Well here is the story, or a piece of it, about my best friend's mother. From the time I became friends with Brian I noticed his mother (Miss Shirley) and how pretty she was. Fast forward several years I was thirty and Brian lived in a different city, he came home for the 4th of July. It was one I would never forget.

"I arrived at Brian's house and his mother was opening the door for other guests, damn she still looked fine as hell. She had to be about 51 or 52 I couldn't remember but she didn't look a day over 40...I was 34.

She gave me a hug as I walked through the door, damn she smelled like an angel. I didn't want to let go of the hug.

She smiled at me and said 'You didn't want to let me go did you,' with a flirty wink. I swallowed hard and just smiled back at her. "Later that day we were playing spades and my partner had to leave and Miss Shirley came over to take her place. We all were having a blast, that's when the fun really began. As the game was going on. I felt something between my legs and looked down to see a perfectly pedicured foot wiggling between my legs. I looked up at her and she smiled and winked. She slowly moved her foot toward my penis and slowly was giving me a dick rub.

"I was turned on and she knew it. I didn't give a damn how or why but I was in heaven. As the game ended her kids came and told her they were making a run to another family member's house. They left and Shirley asked me to help her in the house. "I walked in the house; my eyes were glued to her sundress.

She had my attention and she knew it. Once inside the house she walked in the pantry. After I walked in behind her she closed the door and turned to me and kissed me. All of my dreams years ago were coming true. Was I dreaming or was this real?

"After she kissed me, she put her hands on my shoulders and pushed me to the floor. She lifted her sundress up and exposed her thong to me, she pulled my head towards her body and I began to lick her body through the thong. She moved the thong over to the right side and there it was…the prettiest pussy I had ever seen. I began to eat her like it was the last meal of my life time.

"She was moaning very softly and pushing my head deeper into her thighs. Damn, she even tasted good. I couldn't eat enough, she was about to explode and I felt

a rush of her hot juices hit my chin. Damn, damn,

damn I was more turned on now; I was kissing her clit like it was a cool ice-cream on this hot summer day. She pulled me off my knees and positioned herself by the shelf to allow me to finally make hot love to her.

"I entered her body and couldn't believe how warm and wet she was. I was stroking that ass like Tiger Woods on a golf course. She had another orgasm, then turned around and bent over to tell me to hit it from the back. Her ass was round and nice and smooth. As I entered her body, she squeezed her pussy on my dick and I couldn't hold it any more. I just let go of my nut and pushed every inch of my dick in her and she moaned even louder.

"As I pulled out of her body she looked at me and smiled, I then went back to my knees to begin kissing her legs. I made my way down to her feet and slowly she pulled her feet from her sandals. I sucked on those toes for another ten minutes or so. As I did this the sweat from her was dripping on my head and face. I took my time and the more I sucked, the more she moaned. I don't know if it was the fact that people were walking back and forth and we could hear them that kept the excitement going in that room. "Once we finished she smoothed out her clothes and we walked out of that room with two big smiles. It was a 4th of July I will never, ever forget."

Once he finished Shirley passed around several brochures asking each lady to take one. They all started to read. Shirley got their attention when she told them "This will be our first trip together as a group." She lifted her glass of wine and stated "The Cougar Club is going to the Carribean!" Each lady lifted her glass and they all smiled and said "Here, Here!"

* * * * * * *

Dear Reader,

Well, you're read the first adventure of the Cougar Club. What did you think? Write and express your thoughts. What would you wish for in your initiation? Describe your dream man? Would he be similar to Tyrone or Willie or perhaps your favorite crush? Get your freak on! Close your eyes and fantasize being a member of the Club. For entry, your card please...

Peace. Out. Spread the word.

Stay sexy and

hot!

Dark

Manswellp@yahoo.com

PS: By the way, buy more than one copy of this book. Keep one copy under your pillow and give the other copy to a friend. Don't say I didn't warn you.

Keep reading...I have a surprise for you!!!

Teach your man how to eat your pussy!!

First off, let's have him do

some neck exercises…have

him lean his neck over to

the left then to the

right….now down and

back….if he does this 10 to

15 times a day…his neck

wont get so damn tired or

he wont catch a cramp

when you decide to tighten

up on him for hitting a good

spot. (LOL)

.. ..

Next he needs to practice pushing

his tongue out and in…left to right and up and down….trust me this will help him from cramping up as well….You know you like it when a guy can eat that pussy for long periods of time…without stopping!!! Nothing pisses you off more than when you are about to have a good "NUT" and this fool stops….lolol I know you all have been there.

.. ..

He thinks his two to five minutes of eating you was the bomb and you were just

getting started!

.. ..

Now comes the good parts…he needs to learn how to position not only himself but you also so that you both are comfortable…can't enjoy it if you are not relaxed, am I right?

.. ..

This might help...he needs to have you lay at an angle so that you are good to go and also that he is not leaning too far off the bed. Next he needs to go up to you and

place your legs over his

shoulders like he was

getting dressed…your ass

should be almost at his

chest.

.. ..

Next move is to lock his

arms under your legs but

they should be free to grab

your hands or breast when

the time cums. (I know I am

so Nasty)

.. ..

Now he needs to have his

lips wet just a little, the clit

and pussy lips don't need to

ripped apart by some dry ass chapped lips…once he starts he should get your engine(Pussy) going by licking the lips of your pussy and do this nice and soft…once the juices get going,

then he needs to treat your pussy like your mouth and "French Kiss" it…position his mouth over the pussy and slowly play with the lips and move the tongue around nice and slow. You should be feeling good right about now. (This is where the neck exercises come into play)

.. ..

Next comes the 'clit' he needs to play with his tongue around the clit area until you're just feel like busting a good nut on his face. (This is where the tongue workout comes into play)…this process needs to be done over and over again…he should be licking your clit left and right up and down….if he is taking his time, you should be loving this right about now…he needs to repeat this over and over and over and over and over again…he should feel this is his only mission and when you feel as though you can't take any more and start trying to move his head away because your clit is on fire and you are ready to fuck…then he should grab your hands and lock them by

your side…he should eat you until he is tired of you cumming on his face…if he is really good he will take several more orgasms from you…he should have you thinking about him eating you hours after he is done.

.. ..

He should learn how to breath as well...learn how to lean his head to the left and right to get air…once he gets this...you will get hours of pleasure even if you push his head into your pussy he will know how to get air.

.. ..

You should no longer settle for one orgasm while he is eating and if he is not doing it right…TELL HIM!! You should be enjoying this…not waiting for him to stop and hope you get one later!!

Yours in Heat and Hot Sex,

Dark Chocolate

www.ingramcontent.com/pod-product-compliance
Lightning Source LLC
Chambersburg PA
CBHW061648040426
42446CB00010B/1633